To:

From:

Copyright © Goodmood Press. All rights reserved. No part of this publication may be reproduced, stored in a retrieval system, or transmitted in any form or by any means, electronic, mechanical, photocopying, recording, or otherwise, without written permission of the publisher

Reasons Why I Love You

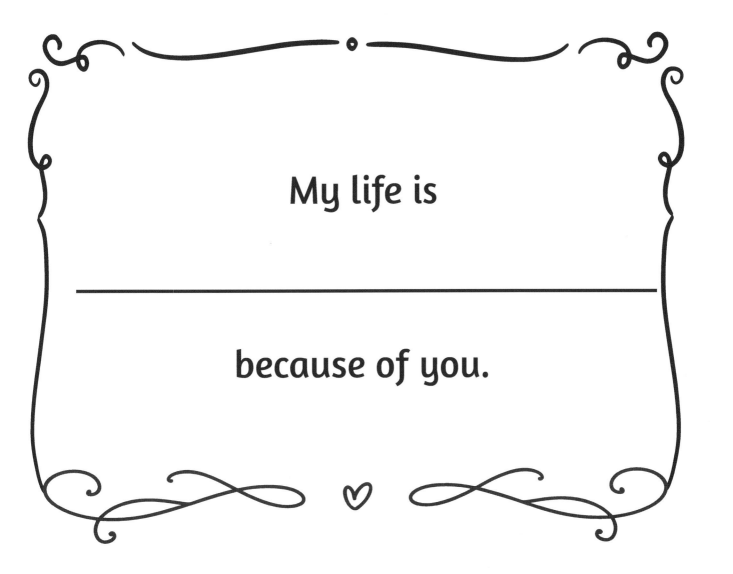

Before you came into my life

_____

You have such a _____ smile

and that smile makes me

_____

You have the cutest

_____

Every time I see you

I love that we both like the same

_____

I love how your voice sounds when

_____

My dreams of you are

_____

When I think about you, I

_____

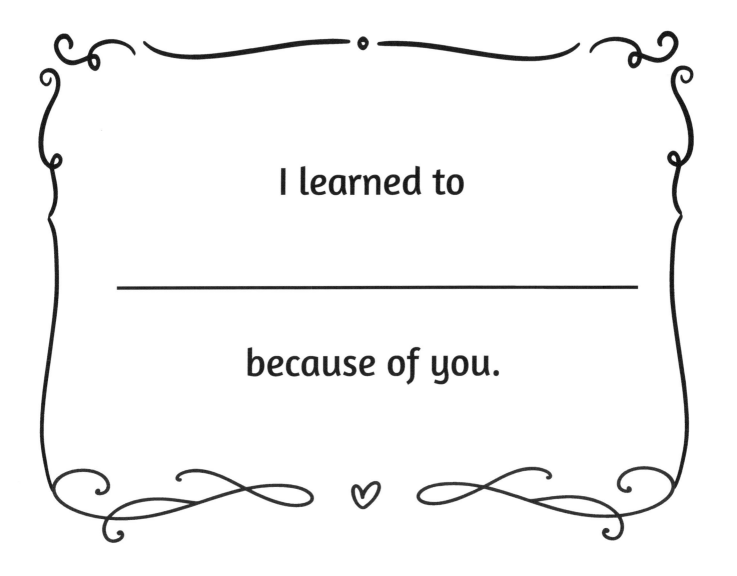

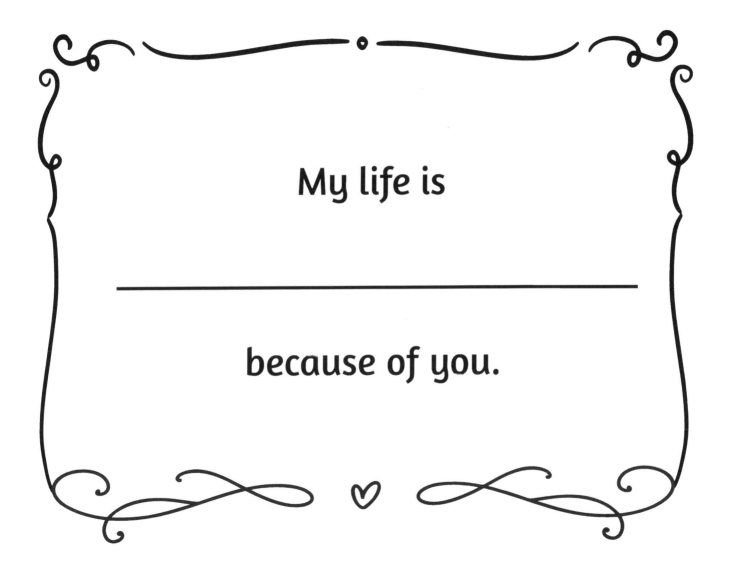

Manufactured by Amazon.ca
Bolton, ON